THE HAND OF THE LORD

Daily Devotions

Matthew D. Rosebrock

CONCORDIA PUBLISHING HOUSE · SAINT LOUIS

Copyright © 2024 Concordia Publishing House
3558 S. Jefferson Ave., St. Louis, MO 63118-3968
1-800-325-3040 • cph.org

Scripture quotations are from the ESV® Bible (The Holy Bible, English Standard Version®), copyright © 2001 by Crossway, a publishing ministry of Good News Publishers. Used by permission. All rights reserved.

Catechism quotations are taken from Luther's Small Catechism
© 1986 Concordia Publishing House. All rights reserved.

Manufactured in the United States of America

1 2 3 4 5 6 7 8 9 10   33 32 31 30 29 28 27 26 25 24

ASH WEDNESDAY AND THE DAYS FOLLOWING

Fear God, Not Men

Exodus 1

But the midwives feared God and did not do as the king of Egypt commanded them, but let the male children live. (Exodus 1:17)

Ancient Israel prospered in the land of Egypt because the hand of the Lord was with them. However, the land that had once been a place of refuge with Joseph became a place of bondage. Pharaoh was losing his grip and ordered the killing of Hebrew newborn boys. But Shiphrah and Puah feared God and not Pharaoh, and so let the children live.

Fear of the world is driven by fleeting threats and false promises. But the fear of God is different. As He calls us to live according to His commandments, God brings about holy fear in us through His Law to recognize that He alone is God. Worldly fear can only drive to despair, but holy fear drives toward repentance and faith, which is supplied only by the Gospel—for Jesus has redeemed us by His blood and righteousness on the cross.

Like Shiphrah and Puah, fearing God and not men means that we have no need to let the world dictate our lives by its short-lived rewards and threats (Psalm 56:11; Acts 5:29). We do not even need to let our left hand know what our right hand is doing as we seek to love our neighbors in our vocations (Matthew 6:3). For God is merciful in Christ Jesus by the work of His hand alone.

Lord, preserve us when temptations seek to strike misplaced fear into our hearts. Lead us to fear, love, and trust in You above all things. In Jesus' name. Amen.

Drawn from the Water

Exodus 2:1–10

When she could hide him no longer, she took for him a basket made of bulrushes and daubed it with bitumen and pitch. She put the child in it and placed it among the reeds by the riverbank. (Exodus 2:3)

After the midwives refused to fear his hand, Pharaoh ordered that all Hebrew newborn male children be cast into the Nile. But with loving hands, Moses' mother refashioned a basket into a floating ark of safety for her young son. Ironically, Pharaoh's own daughter drew Moses from the water. While human hands are at work, the hand of the Lord is at work over this entire situation. Our Lord has a habit of saving through water. He also saved Noah and his family by placing them in an ark, sealing it, and saving them through the deadly waters of the flood.

Though it may look like a mere human hand pouring water upon the head, God's hand is at work in Holy Baptism. He saves us through water and Word as we are united to Jesus' death and resurrection (Romans 6:1–11). For God cleanses us of our sins. Our old sinful self has been drowned in those waters, and we have been drawn from the water into a new life in Christ. Furthermore, the Lord safely places us in the "holy ark of the Christian Church" (*LSB*, p. 269), where we are sealed until the day of Christ's coming.

Dear heavenly Father, thank You for saving us through Holy Baptism. Keep us in Your holy ark, the church, by Your saving hand. In Jesus' name. Amen.

God Remembers the Covenant He Cut

Exodus 2:11–25

And God heard their groaning, and God remembered His covenant with Abraham, with Isaac, and with Jacob. God saw the people of Israel—and God knew. (Exodus 2:24–25)

When Moses witnessed the suffering of his own people at the hands of the Egyptians, he recklessly tried to take matters into his own hands and soon found himself on the run. Still, the Lord was with him, providing for him. Even after the rule of Egypt changed hands, God saw the suffering of His people. He remembered the covenant He had cut with Abraham, Isaac, and Jacob, and He was about to enact His plan of rescue by His hand.

Taking matters into our own hands rarely results in what we think it should, much less does it fix the problems of this world. More often, doing so only makes matters worse. When it comes to our salvation, there is nothing that we can do to earn it. It is completely out of our hands. Our only hope is in the one who has all things in His control. God knows the plight of His people and has sent Jesus to be our Savior, who wins for us the forgiveness of sins. His hand alone will see us through the trials of this day in patience and peace as we trust in His promises to save.

Dear Lord, we praise You for taking our salvation into Your own hands to do what we were never able to do. In Jesus' name. Amen.

The Mighty Hand of the Lord

Exodus 3

So I will stretch out My hand and strike Egypt with all the wonders that I will do in it; after that he will let you go. (Exodus 3:20)

Pharaoh's death grip on God's people was tight, and he would respond only to a mighty hand. Israel was unable to free themselves from his grip, but God's mighty hand can do what no mere human can. For not only will Israel be set free, but also Egypt will hand over their gold and silver as they leave.

We all would be lost in captivity to the devil were it up to the strength of our own hands. Jesus says that the devil is like a strong man who seeks to hold us captive by his strength. However, when Christ came, He cast out demons, signaling that He has come to bind the strong man. He has come as the mighty hand of God to free us from bondage. Christ has plundered the devil's house (Matthew 12:29). Jesus has conquered the devil in order to win us and bring us under His gracious reign. He alone is the mighty hand of God, who fights for us and frees us to live under His reign.

Dear heavenly Father, thank You for sending Jesus to be the mighty hand of God to bind the devil, plunder his house, and bring us to live under Your kingdom forever. In Jesus' name. Amen.

LENT
WEEK ONE

God's Power through Human Hands

Exodus 4

And the LORD said to Moses, "When you go back to Egypt, see that you do before Pharaoh all the miracles that I have put in your power." (Exodus 4:21)

Moses' request for the Lord to show His powerful hand was just as much for himself as it was for the sake of convincing Israel that he came with God's authority. The Lord graciously gave Moses signs, using the staff in his hand—Moses' own hand—and the Nile River to do so. Still, Moses questioned his ability to speak and failed to circumcise his son as God had commanded. However, even with Moses' reluctance, the Lord was about to accomplish what He set out to do.

The power of the Lord's hand does not depend upon human hands to work His signs and wonders. If anything, Moses' weakness simply showcases that the power resides in God alone. This ought to give us confidence in our vocations that God can and does accomplish what He sets out to do with us as His instruments in the world, sometimes even in spite of us. He gets all of the glory. Above all, His glory is shown in weakness. For Christ on the cross looks like weakness to this world, but in fact, it is the power of God's salvation for all who believe (1 Corinthians 1:18).

Dear heavenly Father, help me to trust in Your power alone to accomplish Your purposes. In Jesus' name. Amen.

A Heavy-Handed World

Exodus 5:1–6:1

But the LORD said to Moses, "Now you shall see what I
will do to Pharaoh; for with a strong hand he will send
them out, and with a strong hand he will drive them
out of his land." (Exodus 6:1)

When Moses and Aaron came bearing the Word of the Lord, Pharaoh only tightened his grip on God's people, commanding them to make bricks without straw. The situation was so dire that Israel's leaders saw this promise of freedom as putting the sword into hands of the Egyptians to kill them (Exodus 5:21). However, the hand of the Lord was still in control, as He would use Pharaoh's own hand to send His people out of captivity.

Sometimes when we speak the truth in love, trials only increase. But we ought not to lose hope, for everything is in the Lord's hand (2 Corinthians 6:4–10). If He can use hard-hearted Pharaoh for His purpose of rescuing His people, He certainly will bring us through moments of trial and suffering for His name's sake. For He is drawing us closer to Himself to trust in His merciful care. Christ is no stranger to suffering; His death on the cross brought atonement for our sins. Even though the world may rage, we trust that ultimately the victory is the Lord's because Christ has already risen from the dead for us.

Dear heavenly Father, help us to trust in moments of trial
that Jesus' victory is already secure, just as He lives today. In
Jesus' name. Amen.

An Outstretched Arm

Exodus 6:1–13

I will redeem you with an outstretched arm and with great acts of judgment. (Exodus 6:6)

The arm of the Lord, similar to the hand of the Lord, demonstrates His great might as the only true God, who remembers His covenant with Abraham, Isaac, and Jacob. When the Lord exercises His holy arm for all to see, it is for both salvation and judgment. For Pharaoh, it was judgment against his stubborn refusal to let God's people go. However, for Israel, it was the arm of salvation to bring them freedom from captivity.

When Christ returns, it will likewise be both judgment and salvation. The Lord's justice will be done against all wickedness and against those who stubbornly reject Him. However, this is not a day of fear for those whose trust is in Him. Christ's mighty and outstretched arm is the arm that saves. Christ outstretched His arms upon the cross and received the wrath of God against all sin. This atoned for our sins. Through His Word, that outstretched arm of salvation reaches to each of us to deliver His benefits: forgiveness, life, and salvation.

Dear, heavenly Father, thank You for the holy outstretched arms of Jesus upon the cross, which have brought us redemption. In Jesus' name. Amen.

Not Just a Handful of Names
Exodus 6:14–30

These are the Aaron and Moses to whom the Lord said: "Bring out the people of Israel from the land of Egypt by their hosts." (Exodus 6:26)

Genealogies in the Scriptures are not just a handful of names to be passed over. Each of the names of God's faithful represents a real person who lived and died, had faith and faltered. Genealogies show that God's work is situated in history. The history matters. The names matter. But the Scriptures are not merely a history book; they are the Word of God, through which the Holy Spirit speaks today into the lives of real people. This genealogy is a testament to Moses and Aaron's place in the people of God as of the tribe of Levi.

In Luke's Gospel account (3:23–38), Jesus' genealogy goes all the way back to Adam to testify to the fact that He is the promised off-spring who has defeated the devil and brought redemption through His death and resurrection. In Holy Baptism, God calls each of us by name to be baptized into the triune name of God. Jesus, our Good Shepherd, knows each of us by name, and He calls us and leads us by His protective hand (John 10:3). Furthermore, by faith in Jesus, we each have our name written in the Book of Life (Luke 10:20; Philippians 4:3; Revelation 3:5). God still cares about real names and the people behind them, including you.

Dear Jesus, thank You for calling me by name and placing Your name upon me. Help me to glorify Your name in all that I say and do. Amen.

The Lord Shows His Hand

Exodus 7:1–13

The Egyptians shall know that I am the LORD, when I
stretch out My hand against Egypt and bring out the
people of Israel from among them. (Exodus 7:5)

Pharaoh said that he did not know the Lord. He sees only his own hands, the hands that seemingly hold everything under his thumb. However, such an attitude will not last for long. Pharaoh will know who the Lord is after He stretches out His hand over the land of Egypt.

It can be disheartening when we look upon the world and see the hands of the world at work. They appear all too powerful. We can become frustrated when we do not see the Lord acting in the immediate way that we want from Him. However, we are called to patience and suffering in this life, trusting in the Lord's mighty hand, which will be stretched out to bring righteousness and rescue to us. Jesus has already won for us the victory through His death and resurrection, which has brought us forgiveness and secured for us the victory over the grave. One day, no one will be able to deny that Jesus is the Lord and that He is the hand of the God at work.

Dear heavenly Father, help us to trust in Your timing and
the work of Your mighty, outstretched hand in Jesus. In His
name. Amen.

Blood, Frogs, and Gnats

The Finger of God

Exodus 7:14–8:19

Then the magicians said to Pharaoh, "This is the finger of God." (Exodus 8:19)

Although Pharaoh's magicians could give the semblance of the first two plagues of blood and frogs, they quickly realized that the deeds of the Lord's hand were out of their grasp. They had to conclude that this indeed was the finger of God that had knocked down their displays of power like a house of cards. But this was still not enough to make hard-hearted Pharaoh listen.

People today, likewise, can be impressed—and deceived—by worldly displays of grandeur. The best that the devil can do is a poor imitation of the power of the Lord. However, it all comes to an end the moment the shadows and mirrors fall away to show the devil's deception. Our Lord has come and has exposed the enemy's sleight of hand. For, by the finger of God, He cast out demons (Luke 11:20). He overpowered the devil in order to rescue His people from captivity. He has done it by looking powerless upon the cross—but therein is the power of God to save! Surely, this is the finger of God!

Dear heavenly Father, thank You that Jesus has defeated the devil and rescued us in order to be with You forever. Help me to hold fast to Your Word. In Jesus' name. Amen.

Flies, Dead Livestock, and Boils

The Hand of the Lord Falls with a Severe Plague

Exodus 8:20–9:12

Let My people go, that they may serve Me. For if you refuse to let them go and still hold them, behold, the hand of the LORD will fall with a very severe plague. (Exodus 9:1–3)

Pharaoh thought that he held the Lord's people in his hand when he continually cheated them with false promises. The plagues only intensified as the hand of the Lord fell severely upon Egypt with swarms of flies, dead livestock, and boils. Yet, Israel was spared. Pharaoh was without excuse for his continued refusal. God won the victory over Pharaoh and his false gods.

The devil holds an oppressive hand over this world. He seeks nothing but to cheat God's people, who were created for life. But Jesus says that "the ruler of this world is judged" (John 16:11). God's severe hand of judgment will fall upon all wickedness on the Last Day. Mercifully, as God's people by faith, we have already passed through judgment into life because the wrath of God was poured out upon Jesus on the cross (John 5:24). This means that all who are united to Him in Holy Baptism are shielded from the hand of judgment and are welcomed with open arms into life eternal (Titus 3:5–7).

Dear heavenly Father, thank You for sending Jesus, who received the judgment that we deserve. Give us confidence for the future as we trust in Him. In Jesus' name. Amen.

LENT
WEEK TWO

Hail, Locusts, and Darkness

The Earth Is in the Lord's Hands

Exodus 9:13–10:29

Moses said to him, "As soon as I have gone out of the city, I will stretch out my hands to the Lord. The thunder will cease, and there will be no more hail, so that you may know that the earth is the Lord's." (Exodus 9:29)

When Moses lifted up his hands to heaven, it showed that the Lord's hand was with him. Hail struck down man, beast, and crops. Locusts consumed whatever crops were left. Darkness covered Egypt. These plagues all showed that the Lord of Israel is the Lord of all creation. All the world is the creation of His hands. He has formed it all, and He holds it all together. Pharaoh himself is a creature, and his might simply does not compare.

All of God's creation is beyond our control. But this is not so with Jesus. After Jesus walked on water and rebuked the wind and the waves, everything became calm (Matthew 14:22–33). He showed that all of creation is in His hands. Jesus is the Lord of all creation. Jesus is God in the flesh. This same Jesus is our Savior, who was crucified and raised for us. That means that nothing in all of creation, including rulers, can separate us from the love of God in Christ Jesus (Romans 8:38–39).

Dear heavenly Father, help us to trust that all things are in Your hands, even our very salvation. In Jesus' name. Amen.

The Final Plague Is at Hand

Exodus 11

Then the LORD said to Moses, "Pharaoh will not listen to you, that My wonders may be multiplied in the land of Egypt." (Exodus 11:9)

Pharaoh knew the impending judgment of death to the firstborn well before the first nine plagues, but he only hardened his heart (Exodus 4:23). Even with all of these wonders, Pharaoh still refused to believe. But Pharaoh's hard heart only served to multiply the wonders of the Lord's hand to save His people. For everything is in His hands.

The miraculous wonders of the Lord's hand are not what change people's hearts from unbelief to belief. They did not do so for Pharaoh, and the same is true today. The wonders are done in order to confirm the Word spoken, which has been present all along. So also it is with Jesus' miracles in the New Testament. We do not need to see the signs and wonders to believe today. We have everything that we need in the Word of the Lord. The Word comes to us today with the Lord's mercy in Christ's forgiveness won through His death and resurrection. So the church proclaims the Word today. By God's grace, He brings people from unbelief to belief by the power of the Holy Spirit through the Word (Romans 10:17).

Dear heavenly Father, help me to ever trust that Your Word is more than enough to bring me forgiveness, life, and salvation in Christ. In His name. Amen.

Eating with Staff in Hand

Exodus 12:1–28

In this manner you shall eat it: with your belt fastened,
your sandals on your feet, and your staff in your hand.
And you shall eat it in haste. It is the Lord's Passover."
(Exodus 12:11)

The Passover is a meal ready for a journey, with staff in hand. It is a meal on the eve of salvation, when the Lord will pass over His people, sparing the firstborn and saving them from the hands of Pharaoh.

When Jesus celebrated the Passover on Holy Thursday, it also was a meal on the eve of the Lord's salvific work. For on Good Friday, Christ became the once-for-all sacrificial lamb that takes away the sin of the world (John 1:29). He is the one who traveled the path to the cross in order to atone for our sins.

We are a people on the journey of faith. However, when we partake of the Lord's Supper, Jesus feeds us with His very body and blood and delivers the salvation that He has already accomplished. It is also for strengthening our faith for the journey as we await His second coming. Judgment will pass over us because we have been covered by the blood of the Lamb. Today, the Lord is leading us in the way of truth until the Last Day.

Dear Jesus, thank You for delivering the gift of Your body and blood in the Lord's Supper to us. Help us to follow You, for You are the way, and the truth, and the life. Amen.

The Hand of Judgment and Salvation
Exodus 12:29–42

Then [Pharaoh] summoned Moses and Aaron by night
and said, "Up, go out from among my people, both
you and the people of Israel; and go, serve the Lord, as
you have said. Take your flocks and your herds, as you
have said, and be gone, and bless me also!" (Exodus
12:31–32)

The hand of the Lord's judgment upon Egypt was simultaneously the hand of the Lord's salvation for Israel. These are the two sides of His hand. The same hand that knocks down the proud is the hand that tenderly gathers up His people to free them of slavery. Pharaoh would respond only to the strong hand. How quickly he and all of Egypt's hands that had sought to push God's people down into slavery were now pushing them away into freedom, even handing them Egypt's wealth on the way out.

There are two sides to the hand of our Lord. This will become evident on the Last Day, when Christ will return in judgment. But it is not only a day of judgment. It is also the day of salvation for all who put their trust in Him. For Christ has already defeated our captors of sin, death, and the devil through His death and resurrection. They do not have any hold over us. He has plundered Satan's house, taking all the captives to live in the freedom of His reign forever (Matthew 12:29). This is truly only because of the Hand of the Lord.

Dear heavenly Father, thank You for sending Jesus to be our Savior, who has freed us from the captivity to sin, death, and the devil. In Jesus' name. Amen.

Hand This Down

Exodus 12:43–13:16

It shall be as a mark on your hand or frontlets between your eyes, for by a strong hand the LORD brought us out of Egypt. (Exodus 13:16)

Israel has just been driven out by the hands of the Egyptians. Still, on the way, the Lord instructed them to teach their children in generations to come about what the strong hand of the Lord had done. The people are to hand down these things. From generation to generation, this remembrance is to be more than just a memory. It is a participation in the Lord's salvific events. Handing down this meal is about life and death.

As God's people today, we have been so blessed to have the Gospel of Christ's forgiveness handed down to us from previous generations. They could not but hand down the Lord's grace and mercy to the next generation. Christ has died and risen for the sake of all peoples across the world—past, present, and future. So the Lord also calls us to hand it down to the next generation in our homes and congregations. It is more than just a memory; it is a matter of life and death. For Christ died, and behold, He lives.

Dear heavenly Father, thank You for those who have handed down Your Holy Gospel to us. Use us to share it with the next generation. In Jesus' name. Amen.

The Hand That Leads

Exodus 13:17–22

And the LORD went before them by day in a pillar of
cloud to lead them along the way, and by night in a
pillar of fire to give them light, that they might travel
by day and by night. The pillar of cloud by day and the
pillar of fire by night did not depart from before the
people. (Exodus 13:21–22)

The guiding hand of the Lord led His people in the way of safety.
The route may have seemed circuitous, but the Lord was always acting
to protect His people Israel. He was not leading His people out of the
land of Egypt so that they would perish in the wilderness, but that
they would ultimately defeat their captors. The Lord did not promise
that Israel would never encounter trials, but He did promise that He
would lead them through them.

There are times when this journey of life feels like we are traveling
in circles and are surrounded by danger on all sides. The Lord does
not promise that we will never face hardship or hurt or pain. However, He is not about to remove His eternally protective and guiding
hand from our lives. Jesus is the one who has led the way. He led the
way all the way to the cross, where He won forgiveness. Because He is
raised, He also leads the way to resurrection life. Jesus does not only
show us the way. He *is* "the way, and the truth, and the life" (John
14:6).

Dear heavenly Father, help me to trust that Your leading and
protective hand will never abandon me. You lead me to eternal life in Jesus. In His name. Amen.

The Hand That Parted the Waters

Exodus 14

> Then Moses stretched out his hand over the sea, and the Lord drove the sea back by a strong east wind all night and made the sea dry land, and the waters were divided. And the people of Israel went into the midst of the sea on dry ground, the waters being a wall to them on their right hand and on their left. (Exodus 14:21–22)

While Moses' hand was stretched out over the sea, it was the power of the Lord's hand that parted the waters. The Lord's hand set up walls on each side of the people as He led Israel through the waters on dry ground. But after they passed safely through, those waters came crashing down on Pharaoh's army.

The Lord normally uses the human hand of the pastor to pour water upon the head of the baptized as he says the words "I baptize you in the name of the Father and of the Son and of the Holy Spirit." However, those are the Lord's words, and it is truly the hand of the Lord that makes Baptism what it is by the power of the Word (Matthew 28:19). In Holy Baptism, we pass through the waters and are delivered from our captivity to sin, death, and the devil. For we have been united to Christ Jesus' death and resurrection (Romans 6:1–11).

Dear heavenly Father, thank You for Holy Baptism. For You have brought me through those waters and united me to Jesus forever. In His name. Amen.

LENT
WEEK THREE

Breaking Out in Song

Exodus 15:1–21

Your right hand, O Lord, glorious in power, Your right hand, O Lord, shatters the enemy. (Exodus 15:6)

With immense joy, Moses broke out in song over the Lord's victorious right hand. His sister, Miriam, also joined in, with tambourine in hand, singing to the Lord. Moses and Miriam were singing even before they arrived at their destination. The might of Pharaoh, his officers, and his host were no match for the hand of the Lord, who brought home the victory as He led His people to the home promised to them.

In much the same way, the Lord uses our hymnody today like songs of victory on the battlefield. Though we still daily encounter battles against our own sins and the sorrow of death, Jesus has already come and won the war. His mighty right hand has brought us through the waters of Holy Baptism, where we have died to sin and been raised to newness of life. The victory is already ours. One day, those who have died in the Lord will be raised, and those who are still alive in the Lord will be changed. So let us sing of His mighty right hand of victory today!

Dear heavenly Father, thank You for the victory that we have in Christ. Help me to sing of Your glorious right hand to save today. In Jesus' name. Amen.

The Hand That Feeds

Exodus 15:22–16:36

Let an omer of [manna] be kept throughout your generations, so that they may see the bread with which I fed you in the wilderness, when I brought you out of the land of Egypt. (Exodus 16:32)

Israel went from singing of the great power of the Lord's right hand to grumbling about how much better it would have been to die by the Lord's hand in Egypt. They bristled against the hand that saved them, soon doubting that the Lord would lead them to the Promised Land. Still, the Lord did not leave them, but He mercifully made bitter water sweet and fed them with manna and quail from heaven.

How quickly we can forget how the Lord's right hand has shown itself for us in the past. When trials come up, we may soon find ourselves grumbling against the Lord at our situation, wondering if He cares. Yet the Lord is patient and merciful with us. He is faithful even when we are not. This does not mean that our trials will immediately be removed. But it does mean that the Lord who died and rose for us promises to hold us in His hand. He continues to feed us with His very body and blood in the Holy Supper to sustain us for the journey. "He who calls you is faithful; He will surely do it" (1 Thessalonians 5:24).

Dear Jesus, thank You for feeding us and sustaining us for the journey with Your Word and Sacrament. Amen.

Water from the Stricken Rock

Exodus 17:1–7

"Behold, I will stand before you there on the rock at
Horeb, and you shall strike the rock, and water shall
come out of it, and the people will drink." And Moses
did so, in the sight of the elders of Israel. (Exodus 17:6)

When Moses struck the rock, out flowed water to quench the thirst of grumbling Israel for their journey. The Lord is merciful.

This journey of life can often leave us parched and desiring of anything that will quench our thirst. But Jesus has exactly what we need. Christ encountered a woman at a well who sought to fill her thirst with all the wrong things. However, Jesus freely offered to her "living water . . . welling up to eternal life" (John 4:10–14). Paul says that Christ was the "spiritual Rock" that sustained Israel for their wilderness journey (1 Corinthians 10:4). When the spear struck Christ's side on the cross, out flowed blood and water. His death is life-giving. Christ is the Rock of salvation, who was struck in order to pour out upon us the forgiveness of our sins—our greatest need has been quenched. The Lord continues to hand this to us in Word and Sacrament, "for where there is forgiveness of sins, there is also life and salvation" (Luther's Small Catechism, Sacrament of the Altar, Second Part).

Dear Jesus, thank You for quenching our deepest thirst in Your death on the cross. Because You were struck, we are saved. Amen.

The Lord Is My Banner

Exodus 17:8–16

And Moses built an altar and called the name of it, The
Lord Is My Banner. (Exodus 17:15)

As long as Moses' hands remained stretched up toward the Lord, Israel triumphed over Amalek. Moses' weary uplifted hands in the midst of battle showed Israel that the power and victory is truly in the hands of the Lord. Throughout the Holy Scriptures, the Lord often worked through weakness to show His power to save.

We see the all-too-evident weakness of our own hands. We are incapable of saving ourselves from our battle against sin, death, and the devil. Victory is out of our grasp. But victory is not out of the grasp of our Lord. The church father Cyprian once drew a connection between Moses' elevated hands and the spread-and-nailed hands of Jesus on the cross. Indeed, Christ has done what we could not on His cross. "The cross is folly to those who are perishing, but to us who are being saved it is the power of God" (1 Corinthians 1:18). So the weakness of our hands points all the more to the power of the Lord's hand to save. This is great comfort to us in our daily battles. Paul also says, "When I am weak, then I am strong" (2 Corinthians 12:10). The Lord is my banner!

Dear heavenly Father, help us to trust that in Christ our weakness only magnifies Your power to save. In Jesus' name. Amen.

The Lord's Hand and Using Many Hands

Exodus 18

Jethro said, "Blessed be the LORD, who has delivered you out of the hand of the Egyptians and out of the hand of Pharaoh and has delivered the people from under the hand of the Egyptians. Now I know that the LORD is greater than all gods, because in this affair they dealt arrogantly with the people." (Exodus 18:10–11)

Jethro came to see that the God of Israel is the true God. It was the Lord's hand alone that brought Israel out from under the hand of Egypt. At the same time, the Lord granted Jethro the wisdom to recognize that Moses' tasks were too heavy for him to carry alone. Rather, he needed to entrust others to share the burden and oversee the many responsibilities concerning the people.

Christ has come to bring to us salvation by the power of His hand alone. He, unlike Moses, does not need us to lighten His load. However, He still graciously chose to call disciples to follow Him and proclaim His Word. But the apostles saw the need to delegate responsibilities so that they could devote themselves to preaching the Word (Acts 6:1–7). Your pastor is called to the unique ministry of preaching the Word and administering the Sacraments. At the same time, he cannot bear the heavy load of everything in the congregation. Pastor and congregation are blessed when they see the value and need for "all hands on deck" in the ark of the church. For it is a beautiful thing when the whole congregation folds their hands in prayer and then puts their hands into service while the pastor diligently attends to his call to care for souls.

Dear heavenly Father, help me to see the ways that I can support my pastor(s) and the ministry of my congregation for the sake of the Gospel. In Jesus' name. Amen.

Treasured in the Hand of the Lord

Exodus 19

You shall be My treasured possession among all peoples, for all the earth is Mine; and you shall be to Me a kingdom of priests and a holy nation. (Exodus 19:5–6)

With great care, the Lord has led the people of Israel to the foot of Mount Sinai, treasuring them in His hand. They are His kingdom of priests, a whole kingdom of people that will serve as His intercessors for the world, and His holy nation, a whole nation set apart from the world for His purposes to proclaim the work of the Lord's hand in the world. Yet, sadly, God's own people, who were set apart, end up rebelling against the Lord's hand.

Christ has come as the true Israelite so that all who are in Him are now "a chosen race, a royal priesthood, a holy nation, a people for His own possession" (1 Peter 2:9). God continues to use His church to proclaim the works of His hands. He has created us. He has redeemed us by the blood of Jesus. He sanctifies us through the work of the Holy Spirit through the preaching of the Word and administration of the Sacraments. God uses His church to be a light in the midst of the darkness of this world to draw others to the saving hand of Jesus. In His protective hands, He will continue to treasure and keep His church to the day of resurrection.

Dear heavenly Father, help us as Your church to be witnesses to the world of Your saving hand in Jesus. In His name. Amen.

The Hand of the Law

Exodus 20

I am the LORD your God, who brought you out of the
land of Egypt, out of the house of slavery. (Exodus 20:2)

The first thing God did after bringing Israel out of Egypt by His mighty hand was to give His Law. In the Ten Commandments, the Lord told His people how their life would be shaped. Their life would center on Him as the only true God. All the commandments flow out of the one true God: their relationship to Him (1–3) and their relationships with one another (4–10).

The Law of God is good. It is the design into which the Lord calls us to live. However, because we are sinners, the Law also always accuses us of where we have fallen short and shows us what sinners deserve, which is judgment and death. In this way, the Law was not given to show us how to achieve salvation by our own efforts. Rather, it shows us our need for a Savior. Thanks be to God that Jesus has come as one under the Law in order to save those under the Law (Galatians 4:4–5). It is only because of the free gift of forgiveness that we even come to love the Law of the Lord, not as a way of gaining salvation but as a way of knowing what a God-pleasing life is. However, as sinners, we need to hear again and again how He has come to forgive.

Dear heavenly Father, help me uphold Your good Law in my life, while I trust that it is by Your work alone in Christ that I am saved. In Jesus' name. Amen.

31

LENT
WEEK FOUR

Set Apart

Exodus 21:1–23:19

Now these are the rules that you shall set before them.
(Exodus 21:1)

The Lord set the people of Israel apart to be a holy people. With this new life, the Lord also gave them a new set of standards on how to live with one another. While some of the rules and regulations for the ancient people of Israel may sound strange to our ears today, it is important to see that these were for God's people at a specific time and place. However, in these statutes, we can see the Lord's heart as He expects Israel to act fairly and in accord with His justice and mercy.

Christ has come and fulfilled the whole of the Law for us as the one true Israelite. While we are not ancient Israel of Exodus, the Lord has still called all who believe in Jesus to be the new Israel by His death and resurrection. Jew and Gentile alike are the people of God because of Jesus. By the Holy Spirit at work through the Word, we are called to live in the new reality of being the people of God as the Spirit bears His fruit through us (Galatians 5:22–23).

Dear heavenly Father, grant me, as one who has been made holy by the blood of Jesus, the fruit of the Spirit in my life and bring those fruit forth in my life. In His name. Amen.

The Hand of the Lord Leading the Way

Exodus 23:20–33

Behold, I send an angel before you to guard you on the way and to bring you to the place that I have prepared. (Exodus 23:20)

The Lord's name is in this angel that will lead God's people to the Promised Land. The people are not to mingle with the other peoples or worship their gods. They are to listen only to God's Word, which this angel speaks. God's Word will lead them in the way that they should go. Israel only needs to listen to these words from God Himself and all of the land will be theirs. We know, however, that Israel ultimately did not listen to the Word of the Lord, and so wandered in the desert for forty years before entering the land of Canaan.

Too often, we seek to lead our own way and follow our own word. But when we ignore the Word of God, we do so to our own peril and become people who are like sheep without a shepherd. However, God has sent to us the Word made flesh. He calls us back into the fold so we may walk in His presence. He has laid down His life for us sheep and taken it up again to bring us into His fold (John 10:18). Our life and truth and way are completely dependent upon the One who is "the way, and the truth, and the life" (John 14:6). With Peter, we rightly say, "Lord, to whom shall we go? You have the words of eternal life" (John 6:68).

Dear Jesus, grant us the Holy Spirit to lead us by Your words each day as we trust in You. Amen.

Covenant Confirmed

Exodus 24

Then Moses and Aaron, Nadab, and Abihu, and seventy
of the elders of Israel went up, and they saw the God of
Israel. There was under His feet as it were a pavement
of sapphire stone, like the very heaven for clearness.
And He did not lay His hand on the chief men of the
people of Israel; they beheld God, and ate and drank.
(Exodus 24:9–11)

Moses threw the blood of the covenant sacrifice upon the altar
and the people. Similar to the angel that had passed over every house
marked with blood, so the Lord did not lay His hand on the elders.
Because the Lord sanctified them by the blood, they ate and drank in
the peace of this covenant as they beheld God.

We could not stand before the Lord without being covered by the
blood of Christ. Yet even today He gives us His blood in the Lord's
Supper. Christ's sacrifice on the cross is the blood that cleanses us eternally as saints who "have washed their robes and made them white in
the blood of the Lamb" (Revelation 7:14). As people covered by the
sacrifice of Christ by faith, behold, the Lord does not lay His hand on
us but feeds us with His very body and blood. By faith in Christ, no
matter how weak our faith may be, this meal heals, brings forgiveness,
and strengthens faith. On the Last Day, we will eat and drink together
in God's presence at the great wedding feast of the Lamb in His kingdom (Revelation 19:6–10).

Dear heavenly Father, thank You for covering me in the blood
of Christ so that I may eat and drink in the presence of Your
altar. In Jesus' name. Amen.

The Lord's Plans and Human Hands

Exodus 25–27

And let them make Me a sanctuary, that I may dwell in their midst. (Exodus 25:8)

The Lord's strong hand has led His people out of Egypt, given them His Commandments, and established His covenant with them. Now the Lord lays out the blueprints for the ark of the covenant, furniture, tabernacle, altars, and court. He lays out the materials and designs exactly to His specifications for a place that is befitting of His presence. God does not need human hands to make a tabernacle for His dwelling. However, He graciously condescends to dwell among Israel. The Lord is thus instructing His own people how to use their hands and resources for His service, while it is His presence alone that brings life to this place.

The greatest fulfillment of the Lord's presence comes to us in Christ. God is present in an intimate and special way, unlike anything else in all of history. Both God and man, Jesus saves us from our sinful condition. He does not need the work of our hands to be present among us and in the world. But He still comes to us for our benefit in Word and Sacrament. Furthermore, Jesus dwells in our hearts today by faith in His words (Ephesians 3:17). He makes our hearts the abode of His presence and uses our hands for the sake of serving our neighbors in this life.

Dear Jesus, thank You for being present among us in Word and Sacrament. Use our hands for Your service in the world, and use our mouths to proclaim Your Gospel. Amen.

Woven Priestly Garments

Exodus 28

And you shall make holy garments for Aaron your brother, for glory and for beauty. You shall speak to all the skillful, whom I have filled with a spirit of skill, that they make Aaron's garments to consecrate him for My priesthood. (Exodus 28:2–3)

These garments "for glory and for beauty," made by skilled hands, were to cover the Lord's priesthood in the presence of the Lord with the symbols for the whole people Israel. The coverings were both for the priests' intercession on behalf of the people and for their protection before the holiness of the Lord. These consecrated garments were a constant reminder that this was the Lord's priesthood and that it was the Lord who made them holy.

This covering of the Old Testament priesthood foreshadowed the priesthood of Christ. Christ has given Himself as the perfect sacrifice for our sins through His blood shed on the cross. He has thus removed our need for the temporal priesthood of the Old Testament. In Holy Baptism, we are clothed with Christ and His righteousness. We can go before our Father in heaven with confidence because we are covered by Christ (Hebrews 4:16).

Dear heavenly Father, thank You for clothing me in Christ. Help me to let all my requests be made known because of Him. In Jesus' name. Amen.

Consecrated Priests

Exodus 29–30

There I will meet with the people of Israel, and it shall be sanctified by My glory. I will consecrate the tent of meeting and the altar. Aaron also and his sons I will consecrate to serve Me as priests. I will dwell among the people of Israel and will be their God. And they shall know that I am the Lord their God, who brought them out of the land of Egypt that I might dwell among them. I am the Lord their God. (Exodus 29:43–46)

The Lord established the tabernacle and priesthood as a way of mediating His holiness so that He might dwell among His people. The Lord instructed Moses that before the priests could utilize their hands for work within the sanctuary of the Lord, sacrifices needed to be made. But sacrifices did not stop at ordination. Continual sacrifices and rituals before the Lord were necessary for the service of the tabernacle to be acceptable in the sight of the Lord.

In order to stand before the Lord, we need someone to intercede for us. The Old Testament priesthood, however, was only a shadow of Christ's priesthood. Christ did not need to make sacrifices for Himself (Hebrews 5:1–10). His sacrifice was for us. Christ comes from the eternal order of Melchizedek (Hebrews 5:6; 7:1–3, 15–22). He is both the priest and the eternal sacrifice that is once for all time (Hebrews 9:11–15, 24–28; 10:12–14). Christ shed His blood upon the cross as the perfect sacrifice for the whole world's sins. He alone is our intercessor.

Dear heavenly Father, thank You for Jesus, our great High Priest, whose sacrifice has made us acceptable in Your sight. In His name. Amen.

The Hands of the Artists

Exodus 31:1–11

The LORD said to Moses, "See, I have called by name Bezalel the son of Uri, son of Hur, of the tribe of Judah, and I have filled him with the Spirit of God, with ability and intelligence, with knowledge and all craftsmanship, to devise artistic designs, to work in gold, silver, and bronze, in cutting stones for setting, and in carving wood, to work in every craft." (Exodus 31:1–5)

All of the plans for the tabernacle, its furniture, and the priestly garments have been laid out as the Lord had commanded. Now He declares how He will bring them into fruition. He blessed some men with the know-how, abilities, and skills to fashion items according to His plans for the tabernacle, in which He would be present with His people.

While the nature of Bezalel and Oholiab's artistic vocations were unique to them alone, the Lord still does bless some men and women with the knowledge, abilities, and skills to work with His creation in beautiful ways. Our sin easily corrupts all of God's gifts, all that was meant to be good, turning each in on itself. Our ugly sin can even masquerade as "beauty." Yet Christ took our sin upon Himself on the cross in order to pour out His beautiful love, which redeems us. As such, the Lord can and still does use artists and craftsmen to testify to our God, who creates, redeems, and sanctifies. Moreover, art within the sanctuary can serve as continual reminders and instruction that derive from and point back to God's Word. Blessed be our beautiful Lord and Savior, Jesus.

Dear Jesus, thank You for taking our ugly sin upon the cross in order to pour out Your beautiful saving love for us. Amen.

LENT
WEEK FIVE

Hands at Rest and the Finger of God

Exodus 31:12–18

And He gave to Moses, when He had finished speaking with him on Mount Sinai, the two tablets of the testimony, tablets of stone, written with the finger of God. (Exodus 31:18)

The Lord emphasized again the importance of Sabbath rest. Sabbath rest is tied directly to the Lord, who created the world in six days and rested on the seventh. When Israel rests on the Sabbath, their rest proclaims to the world who the Creator is. It also proclaims that their work is not what ultimately sustains them. Rather, it is God, by whose finger this commandment was written.

When Jesus came, He established that true Sabbath rest is in His Word. Christ labored for us during Holy Week to bring us forgiveness, life, and salvation. On the sixth day, Good Friday, He cried out, "It is finished" (John 19:30) and rested on the seventh day, Holy Saturday (John 19:38–42). He rose on Sunday, the first day of a new week (John 20:1), but it is not just any Sunday. It is also the eighth day, the first day of the new creation initiated by Jesus' resurrection from the dead. For new creation is found in Him. We are no longer confined to make Saturday the day of rest, for Sabbath rest is wherever we receive the Word of God. This is not our work, but it is God's work to create for us faith that clings to His promises. Thus it is still appropriate that we should set aside time to rest from the work of our hands so we may gather around the places where the Lord's promises are handed to us in Word and Sacrament.

Dear heavenly Father, help me to trust and rest in Your promises in Christ. In Jesus' name. Amen.

Out of Hand

Exodus 32

As soon as he came near the camp and saw the calf
and the dancing, Moses' anger burned hot, and he
threw the tablets out of his hands and broke them at
the foot of the mountain. (Exodus 32:19)

When Moses took longer than expected up on Mount Sinai, things got out of hand in the camp below. How quickly Israel's impatient hands turned to idol-worshiping hands before a golden calf. When Moses saw it, he threw down the tablets of the Commandments. There, in pieces at the foot of the mountain, lay testament to the fact that Israel had broken the chief commandment: "You shall have no other gods."

Whether in thoughts, words, or the deeds of our hands, at the heart of all sin lies idolatry that fears, loves, and trusts in anything or anyone other than the one true God. (See Luther's explanation of the First Commandment in his Small Catechism.) Any attempts to piece our lives together always fall woefully short. Our salvation is out of our hands, for we have broken God's Law. However, God has taken our salvation up into His hands by sending Jesus, who remained faithful to the point of His death on the cross to atone for the sin of the world (Philippians 2:5–11). Graciously, He takes us up into His hands to wash us of our sins in Holy Baptism. Christ keeps us forever in those hands, out of which no one can snatch us (John 10:28–30).

Dear heavenly Father, thank You for taking up what was out of my hands to forgive and keep me forever. In Jesus' name. Amen.

The Merciful Hand of the Lord

Exodus 33

"But," He said, "you cannot see My face, for man shall
not see Me and live." And the LORD said, "Behold, there
is a place by Me where you shall stand on the rock,
and while My glory passes by I will put you in a cleft of
the rock, and I will cover you with My hand until I have
passed by. Then I will take away My hand, and you shall
see My back, but My face shall not be seen."
(Exodus 33:20–23)

After the idolatry of the golden calf, the Lord warned the people that He would not be going on to the Promised Land with them, for if they were in His presence, He would consume them. Moses knew, however, that the Lord's presence was at the heart of Israel being His people, so He interceded for them. They needed the Lord's hand with them. But sinners in the presence of God in His glory would meet certain death. And Moses also needed the Lord's hand to protect him. Mercifully, the Lord placed His hand over Moses to shield him from seeing the full glory of His face as He gave him a passing glance at His glory.

We, as God's people today, cannot survive without the Lord's merciful hand. God is present with us in Christ. At the same time, as Martin Luther expressed often in his theology of the cross, God has concealed His full glory in His death on the cross so that we are not consumed (see Lamentations 3:22). Rather, "in the cross of Christ I glory" because of the forgiveness that He has won for us there (*LSB* 427). As we live in God's mercy today, "we walk by faith, not by sight" as we await the day of Christ's second coming (2 Corinthians 5:7). "For now we see in a mirror dimly, but then face to face" (1 Corinthians 13:12).

Dear heavenly Father, help us always to see that Your glory is most shown in Christ's cross for us. In His name. Amen.

Hands and Faces

Exodus 34

When Moses came down from Mount Sinai, with the
two tablets of the testimony in his hand as he came
down from the mountain, Moses did not know that
the skin of his face shone because he had been talking
with God. (Exodus 34:29)

In the Lord's mercy, He renewed the covenant with His people. Moses cut new tablets and brought them before the Lord so that His commandments could be inscribed upon them. Moses' own skin reflected the glorious light of being in the presence of the Lord. It shone so much that Moses even needed a protective veil over his face in order to be in the presence of the Lord's people.

When Jesus was transfigured before Peter, James, and John, He appeared on the mountain with Moses and Elijah. Jesus' "face shone like the sun," radiating with the glory of the Lord (Matthew 17:2). Jesus, the Son of God, was the source of the light. He had not come to be another Moses, however. He mercifully reached down and touched the terrified disciples, who were cowering with their faces on the ground. As they then looked up, they saw only Jesus (Matthew 17:6–8). Jesus, the one in whom rests the glory of the Lord, indeed still reaches down to us through His Word to give us His mercy. We are to listen to Him.

Dear heavenly Father, help us to trust in Jesus as the merciful
hand that continues to reach down to us through Your Word.
In Jesus' name. Amen.

The Contributing Hand

Exodus 35:1–29

Take from among you a contribution to the Lord.
Whoever is of a generous heart, let him bring the Lord's
contribution. (Exodus 35:5)

The Lord had given the Israelites all that they had. His mighty hand had brought them out of Egypt. His hand had brought them through the waters. His hand had fed them and given them water to drink. They had an overabundance of gifts from the Lord. Now, they had the opportunity to give freely for the tabernacle.

When we tithe to the ministry of the church, whether for the building or the budget, we do not do so out of compulsion. We cannot ever possibly pay the Lord back for what He has first given us. Rather, our giving flows out of the freedom and trust of knowing that Jesus is the Lord of our lives. God has created us and given us everything we need for this earthly life. He has redeemed us by the blood of Jesus, forgiving all our sins (1 John 1:7). He has called us by the Gospel to believe and receive this forgiveness, life, and salvation. When we give to the Lord, we do so in the trust that the Lord will continue to daily provide for us.

Dear heavenly Father, help us to give freely of that which You have first given us for the sake of Your kingdom. In Jesus' name. Amen.

The Constructing Hand

Exodus 35:30–38:31

Bezalel and Oholiab and every craftsman in whom the LORD has put skill and intelligence to know how to do any work in the construction of the sanctuary shall work in accordance with all that the LORD has commanded. (Exodus 36:1)

Now the construction of the tabernacle began. The Lord gave Bezalel, Oholiab, and every craftsman in Israel's camp both the skills and the plans for the tabernacle to be made exactly to His specifications. The Lord used these craftsmen to bring all His plans to fruition.

The Lord has given to each of us skills and abilities to be used both within our various vocations for service to our neighbors and within the church in support of the proclamation of the Gospel. God does not need our hands to make Him a tabernacle or to accomplish His purposes. God made His presence known in the tabernacle; in Christ, He has made His presence known among us (John 1:14). He has taken on human flesh without sin in order to redeem sinners by His death and resurrection. Therefore, also by His work and presence in our lives, He deigns to use our hands in order to deliver His good gifts to our neighbors.

Dear heavenly Father, thank You for sending Jesus to live among us in order to redeem us. Use our hands to deliver Your gifts to our neighbors and make us ready to proclaim the hope that is within us. In Jesus' name. Amen.

The Consecrating Hand

Exodus 39

And Moses saw all the work, and behold, they had done it; as the LORD had commanded, so had they done it. Then Moses blessed them. (Exodus 39:43)

The ark, the table, and the altars, every woven curtain and tanned skin, every piece of acacia wood overlayed with precious metal, every priestly garment adorned with beauty has now been made and presented to Moses. Everything has been made according to the command of the Lord. Now it is consecrated, set apart for holy use in the Lord's tabernacle, the place that is set apart as where the Lord would live among His people.

The Lord continues to consecrate, to set apart the places where He promises to be found. The Lord continues to bless wherever His Word is spoken, not because the places of themselves have greater significance, but because His Word is spoken there. When we gather in the sanctuary on Sunday, it is a holy place because that is where the Word is. Where the Word is, there is our Savior, coming to impart His gifts of life and salvation to us, won by His once-for-all sacrifice on the cross.

Dear heavenly Father, help us to cherish all the places where Your Word is proclaimed in its truth and sincerity. In Jesus' name. Amen.

HOLY WEEK

The Glory of the Lord Is at Hand

Exodus 40

Then the cloud covered the tent of meeting, and the glory of the Lord filled the tabernacle. (Exodus 40:34)

The glory of the Lord is at hand! The tabernacle has been constructed and erected, the priesthood consecrated, everything situated as the Lord had instructed. Now, at the end of Exodus, the glory of the Lord's presence fills the tabernacle and continues to do so through the years of wandering in the desert to the reign of King David. That same glory of the Lord fills the temple constructed by King Solomon. However, Ezekiel tells us that later, after years of rejection, the glory of the Lord departed from the temple, which was later destroyed (Ezekiel 10:18). After exile, the returning Judeans built a new temple. But it did not have the ark of the covenant or the glory of the Lord. The temple was empty.

Jesus, however, is the fullness of God in the flesh. When Jesus arrived on Palm Sunday, the glory of the Lord was again at hand in His holy city. People threw their cloaks and palm branches on the road and their hands up in praise while Jesus held in His hands the reins of a noble but humble donkey. Jesus would take that presence of God all the way to the cross, where He would die for the sins of the whole world. At the moment of His death, the temple curtain would be torn in two as He made the presence of the Lord available to all believers (Mark 15:38). Even now, His glory is at hand in the humble means of Word and Sacrament.

Dear heavenly Father, help us to see the places where Your glory is present in Word and Sacrament. In Jesus' name. Amen.

Into the Hand of Those Who Strike
Isaiah 50:5–10

I gave My back to those who strike, and My cheeks to those who pull out the beard; I hid not My face from disgrace and spitting. (Isaiah 50:6)

Christ is the Suffering Servant of Isaiah; He did not shrink back from the violent hands of this world. He was struck before the high priest. He was spat on. He was flogged by the Romans. He was struck by the soldiers. He had a crown of thorns pressed into His brow. He was clothed with purple robes and mocked. Christ remained resolute through it all, with His face set "like a flint" (Isaiah 50:7).

The suffering that Christ endured at the hands of sinful men is too much for us to bear. At the same time, those hands are ours as well. Our sin was placed upon Him. However, He willingly suffered, for He knew that He would be vindicated. Christ knew what Easter morning would bring (Mark 8:31–9:1, 30–31; 10:32–34). He knew the victory that He was accomplishing for even the worst of sinners as He took upon His body the very wrath of God against all sin. Even though He did not sin, Christ gave His back to those who strike in order to win us back into the Father's loving embrace.

Dear Jesus, thank You for Your willingness to suffer in our stead. Help us to entrust our whole lives into Your care. Amen.

Hidden in the Shadow of His Hand

Isaiah 49:1–7

He made My mouth like a sharp sword; in the shadow
of His hand He hid Me; He made Me a polished arrow;
in His quiver He hid Me away. (Isaiah 49:2)

When Christ first came into this world, He came in humility. He came as one hidden in the hand of the Father. As a vulnerable little baby, He was protected in Egypt and brought back at the right time. Though He came in humility, with His divine nature hidden by the hand of the Lord, His sharp words pierced the heart as they convicted of sin and brought healing at just the right time.

The Lord continues to come to us through the humble means of His Word and the Sacraments. It is in the Lord's words where the power resides. His words still pierce our hearts today in Law, which convicts us of our sin, and Gospel, which makes us alive in Him. "For the word of God is living and active, sharper than any two-edged sword" (Hebrews 4:12). In the shadow of God's hand, we are hidden; there, our eyes of faith see that the Word of God pointedly kills and makes alive in Christ Jesus.

Dear Lord, keep my heart open to the sharpness of Your Word, which calls me to repentance and faith. In Jesus' name. Amen.

The Only Arm to Bring Salvation and Judgment

Isaiah 62:11–63:7

I looked, but there was no one to help; I was appalled,
but there was no one to uphold; so My own arm
brought Me salvation, and My wrath upheld Me.
(Isaiah 63:5)

Because of sin, this world stands condemned. Our arms are far too weak to bring about salvation to ourselves, let alone to this world. We cannot do it by our own strength. We cannot do it by our own power. However, the Lord has taken matters into His own hands by sending Jesus as our salvation.

Jesus fulfilled these words of Isaiah. Everyone ended up deserting the Lord when His time came. His own disciples could not stay awake while Jesus prayed in the Garden of Gethsemane (Luke 22:39–46). Then they fled. Even Peter denied Jesus three times (Luke 22:54–62). In the moment of trial, Christ was abandoned by all of His disciples as He alone innocently bore the brunt of an unrighteous world.

However, this is the arm of the Lord that brings salvation. His death on the cross is both the pouring out of God's wrath against all sin and salvation for all who are in Him by faith. Christ alone is the one who can bring salvation. Christ alone is the one who has brought salvation.

Dear heavenly Father, help us to trust in You alone as the one to bring us salvation through Your Son and our Lord, Jesus. In His name. Amen.

Lift Up the Cup of Salvation
Psalm 116

I will lift up the cup of salvation and call on the name of the LORD, I will pay my vows to the LORD in the presence of all His people. (Psalm 116:13–14)

As Israel celebrated the Passover in Egypt, the cup that they raised in hand was indeed the cup of salvation. The angel of death passed over their homes, which were marked with blood to note that the Lord was rescuing them from the hand of the Egyptians.

It was at the annual remembrance of this meal, which Jesus celebrated with His disciples on the night when He was betrayed, when He lifted up the bread and said, "This is My body." He took the cup and said, "This is My blood" (see Luke 22:14–23; 1 Corinthians 11:24–25). Because of Jesus' words, that is just what the bread and wine are: His body and His blood. On this day, when we come together to receive Christ's body and blood, Jesus delivers into our mouths His very body and blood for the forgiveness of our sins and the strengthening of our faith. Wherever Jesus is present, there is also forgiveness, life, and salvation.

Dear Lord, prepare our hearts and minds to receive Christ's body and blood in, with, and under the bread and cup on this holy night. In Jesus' name. Amen.

Into Your Hand

Psalm 31

Into Your hand I commit my spirit; You have redeemed me, O Lord, faithful God." (Psalm 31:5)

Entrusting one's life into another's hands is a matter of faith. David knew what it was to have enemies surround him and threaten his life. However, he knew that his Lord was ever faithful and that he resided in the hand of the Lord. The Lord would see him through this trial, as in times past. The Lord and the Lord alone would redeem him, for God is faithful to His promises.

With nails in His hands, Jesus loudly cried out with the words of Psalm 31 (Luke 23:46) shortly before His death on the cross. Jesus humbled Himself to take on human flesh in order to suffer and die in our stead. Indeed, Christ was delivered into the hands of sinful men to be crucified. However, He was in control of His life and how He would die (John 10:18). Jesus entrusted Himself into the hands of the Father, and He was faithful all the way to the point of death, for He also knew what this would bring: life from the grave and redemption for us. Because we are in Christ, our lives are in the hands of our Redeemer.

Dear Lord, help us to entrust our days into Your hands, for we know that Jesus is our Redeemer. In His name. Amen.

Lions' Mouths Held Shut

Daniel 6:1–24

My God sent His angel and shut the lions' mouths, and
they have not harmed me. (Daniel 6:22)

The king reluctantly used the signet ring on his hand to seal
Daniel into the lions' den. Daniel was put in a place that under any
other circumstances would mean certain death. However, the Lord
watched over Daniel and sent His angel to hold shut the mouths of
those consuming lions.

In this life, death is still a reality. Likewise, the effects of death
consume our mortal bodies. But what happens when Christ, the
Righteous One, dies? After Christ died, He was placed into the tomb;
the entrance was covered by a stone and sealed. Under any other circumstances, death would have consumed the body. However, this was
not so with Jesus. After Jesus' death, His body was kept safe in the
tomb without corruption or decay. But He left the tomb long enough
to descend in triumph to the cave of hell to shut the mouth of the
prowling lion, Satan, forever. Then He rose from the dead to also shut
the consuming mouth of death forever for all who believe in Him
(Psalm 16:10). In Holy Baptism, we have been joined to His death
(Romans 6:3). That means that one day, all those who have died in
Christ will be raised to life eternal.

Dear Lord, thank You that Jesus has now shut the mouths
of consuming death and the devil so that they do not have
the final say over us. Turn our hope to the promise of the
resurrection into life eternal for all who are in Jesus. In His
name. Amen.

The Right Hand of the Lord Does Valiantly

Psalm 118:14–29

> The LORD is my strength and my song; He has become my salvation. Glad songs of salvation are in the tents of the righteous: "The right hand of the LORD does valiantly, the right hand of the LORD exalts, the right hand of the LORD does valiantly!" (Psalm 118:14–16)

Jesus Christ is risen today! Alleluia! It is right that we should sing of the Lord's victorious resurrection!

The psalmist quotes from Moses' song of salvation that he sang after the Lord rescued the people of Israel by His mighty hand through the waters of the Red Sea (Exodus 15:1–18). This mighty right hand does valiantly because it is the hand of the Lord. The Lord rescued His people in strength.

This right hand of the Lord continues to be a source of strength that is by our side each and every day because of Christ's resurrection from the dead. This is the moment in which all of history has forever been changed. He has defeated sin, death, and the power of the devil for us. He has brought us through the waters of Holy Baptism, uniting us to His death and resurrection.

Christ is risen! He is risen indeed! Alleluia! Amen.

Dear heavenly Father, thank You that Jesus has overcome death for us on this holy day. Help us to rejoice in His resurrection life every day. In Jesus' name. Amen.